Jump Start Your Discovery Practice for New Lawyers

By Thomas Lowe

Typesetting by FormattingExperts.com

Contents

Introduction 7

Chapter One: Reasons For Discovery 11

    To get evidence 11

    Avoiding surprises 12

    Narrowing the issues 12

    Perpetuating evidence 13

    Perpetuating testimony from outside the state 13

    To Raise the cost 14

Chapter Two: Preparing For Discovery 17

    What is the case all about?—The Deep Issue 17

    You must prove two cases 20

Chapter Three: Black-letter Law 23

    Use Jury instructions 23

    Use Statutes and Case Law for Authority 24

    Research the Defenses 25

    Be Creative 25

    Determine the relevant documents 26

    Determine who has knowledge of facts 28

    List what you can prove now 29

Determine what defenses your opponents can prove now . . 29

Determine what to prove through your opponent or a 3d
party 30

List documents & things from the opposing side & third
parties 30

List witnesses you need to depose 30

List facts for admission and denial 31

List factual questions for interrogatories 32

Chapter Four: Electronic Discovery 33

Instruct your client to preserve all relevant records 34

Ensure that your regular clients have reasonable backup
and destruction policies and enforce them 36

Prepare for the initial discovery conference 37

Use a professional on voluminous data 38

Negotiate for reasonable disclosure 38

Chapter Five: Order Of Discovery 41

Avoid educating the other side 41

Federal - initial disclosure under FRAP 26(a) 41

Ask for documents and things first 43

Who pays for copies and other expenses of discovery? 45

What form should your responses take? 45

Preparing to depose the opposite party 46

Preparing your witnesses for deposition 49

Depositions to preserve testimony 50

Deposition mechanics 52

Conducting a Deposition 56

Interrogatories 57

When to use subpoenas 59

Summary 60

Chapter Six: Approaches To Responding

To Discovery Requests 61

Generally 61

The bare minimum 62

Overwhelm your opponent 63

Impress your opponent 64

The format of discovery responses 66

Serve supplementary responses 67

Chapter Seven: Organizing Discovery Materials 69

Chapter Eight: When The Other Side Doesn't Cooperate . . . 73

Try to settle your differences 74

File a motion to compel 75

Chapter Nine: General Office Practices 77

Log the flow of documents 77

Log phone messages 78

Get your email box to zero by quitting time 80

Concluding Words 85

Appendix A: Instructions To Deponent 87

Appendix B: Software 93

PDF Generation 93

Encryption 93

Outlining 94

Backing Up Your Data 94

If you know the enemy and know yourself, you need not fear the result of a hundred battles. If you know yourself but not the enemy, for every victory gained you will also suffer a defeat.

—Sun Tzu, *The Art of War*, Part III, §18.

Introduction

Several years ago, I had far too much legal work to do in the time I had available. I needed some help, but for a limited period. It occurred to me that the son of a longtime friend had recently graduated from law school and was attempting to open a solo practice out of his apartment. I knew that he would eventually build a decent law practice if he could survive the first year or two. In the meantime, it seemed like I had received the answer to a prayer. I could give him quite a bit of work at a reduced hourly rate, and the client would not object so long as I was supervising him.

I was in for a rude surprise.

Having practiced law for over 30 years, I had forgotten what it was like when I started playing the discovery game with real live clients and real-life cases. Although my young lawyer had studied civil procedure, he had no familiarity with the actual mechanics of discovery, and seldom knew what to do next. He required continual supervision, which made his services far less valuable.

What was so frustrating to me (and to him) was that most of what he didn't know was not terribly complicated or arcane. Learning to ride a bicycle was harder. I finally realized that the law professor that taught him federal procedure, who, incidentally, was a practicing lawyer, had also forgotten the problems he encountered in his early practice. The professor saw no reason to teach the nuts and bolts of actually doing discovery. It was from this epiphany that the idea of this book arose.

This book is intended for lawyers who have recently entered law practice. If you are starting out as an associate, you may find this book somewhat less useful than a solo lawyer, but the trend is away from mentoring. An increasing number of law firms now expect new associates to immediately pull their own weight. This book is written to help the beginning lawyer get ready fast.

All lawyers remember getting caught in a discovery trap and having to give a case away or lose it. In the course of that first case, most beginning lawyers find their encounter with discovery horrible. Wading through the discovery process turned out to be a frustrating and humiliating experience against better-prepared lawyers.

In law school you probably took a course on the Federal Rules of Civil Procedure, but even if you made an A, you almost certainly have found the discovery process in the context of a live case to be highly intimidating. When you begin your practice, almost every other lawyer in the bar will be more experienced than you. Opposing counsel will be aware of your inexperience and will take advantage of it at every possible opportunity.

Unfortunately, discovery, the ostensible purpose of which is to save judicial time and make the parties more inclined to settle before trial, has in nearly every case, served mainly to increase the time and money that must be expended by both sides. While this has been a bonanza for law firms who bill by the hour, it has been a disaster for lawyers who earn their living through personal injury cases, domestic litigation, and other types of practice in which the client does not have virtually unlimited funds to pay for the meticulous discovery that has unfortunately become standard practice. Lawyers can no longer accept small cases, even cases with considerable merit, because the cost of discovery in time and expenses often exceeds any possible recovery.

While there exist large plaintiff law firms with the financial resources to bring class actions, mass torts, and product liability litigation, all of which depend upon extensive discovery, it is a safe assumption, since you are reading this, that you do not belong to this elite fraternity. You have filed or are about to file a complaint. You need quick, practical guidance to navigate the discovery process without running aground or sinking your client's case.

Since state discovery rules vary from state to state, I use the Federal Rules of Civil Procedure, which are uniform and similar to state rules. In both federal and state courts you must also familiarize yourself with local rules of court, which are beyond the scope of this book. Local rules set out procedures that the judges have established for practice in their courts. You will find rules regarding the length of pleadings, the structure of documents you file with the court, filing deadlines, discovery deadlines and procedures—virtually anything that the judges believe facilitates the disposition of cases. While local rules are subordinate to global rules, as a practical matter they will have the same force as the former, and you are obliged to follow them, lest you jeopardize your case and your standing with the judges.

Do not hesitate to ask advice of other lawyers, clerks, law professors, and anyone else who might have familiarity with discovery practices that are particular to your jurisdiction. Other lawyers will usually be happy to help you, and if you feel really inadequate, you can always associate an experienced lawyer and share the fee.

Chapter One

Reasons For Discovery

To get evidence

You must get everything your opponent has. Otherwise, you cannot evaluate the case. You already know this. A new case could be a rough diamond or a dead weight around your neck. Still, there is nothing more exciting to a new lawyer than a live, breathing client who needs your help.

Sometimes clients may mislead. Find out everything you can about your client before you evaluate your case and your opponent's case. *If you believe you have the perfect case, you are wrong.*

A perfect case may exist among the millions of cases filed in the courts each year, but the odds that a perfect case walks in your office are considerably less than the odds of your winning the Publishers Clearing House Sweepstakes. You will have to work to win. If it's an important case involving large sums of money, you will have to work very, very hard.

The discovery process will assist you in finding the strengths and weaknesses in your case, as well as the evidence you need to prove it. The same goes for your opponent. It will also enable you to evaluate your opponent's defenses, if you are the plaintiff.

Avoiding surprises

One oft-stated purpose of discovery is to avoid surprise and to end the practice of trial by ambush. Prior to the introduction of discovery practice, each side marshaled its witnesses and proceeded to trial, often in ignorance of what the other side planned to offer as evidence.

Today, the parties, having gone through the discovery process, have little risk of being blindsided by evidence of which they were unaware.

Narrowing the issues

Most pleading today is notice pleading, which does not require a detailed blow-by-blow description of the facts of the case, but only requires the basic facts that constitute each cause of action. Good attorneys plead every non-frivolous (and often frivolous) theory of the case on the offhand chance that it might be supported by evidence that emerges during the discovery process. Many of those theories, embedded in separate causes of action, will fall by the wayside when it becomes obvious that the facts do not support them.

The issues that remain after discovery will almost always be fewer and narrower, which is usually a good thing.

Occasionally, the facts unearthed in discovery support an additional cause of action or theory of the case. Courts will usually allow a party to amend his complaint or answer to incorporate the new matters.

Perpetuating evidence

Witnesses can move, get sick, or die. Frightened by threats or enticed by substantial bribes, they can tell you one thing and then testify to the opposite in court. Evidence can be hidden or destroyed. Exhibits can deteriorate or disappear in the natural course of nature and events. Businesses destroy records on a routine basis after they reach a predetermined age. Casinos, for example, usually erase videotapes of the gaming rooms after 45 or 90 days, so if you need a tape from a casino to prove your client's whereabouts on a particular evening, you must move quickly.

Perpetuating testimony from outside the state

If there is a critical witness who lives in another state, it will be necessary to follow the procedure of the state of residence to depose the witness. If the deposition gives all sides the opportunity to examine and cross-examine the witness, then the testimony of the witness is admissible in court, the same as any other witness. It is advisable to videotape the deposition, as juries tend to become bored with testimony read to them from the witness stand.

You can conduct an audio deposition over Skype or the telephone. Make sure that your deponent is sworn by a notary public with authority where the deponent will give the deposition. Afterward, have your secretary transcribe the recording. You will also need a written certification from the notary public attesting that she swore in the witness for the deposition.

To Raise the cost

Discovery costs money and time. The more discovery, the more money the parties must spend to prepare discovery requests and to comply with discovery requests from other parties. Your opponent, by not cooperating, can gobble up your time filing and arguing motions to compel, and courts are often unwilling to sanction the offending party with more than a modest slap on the wrist.

In all but the simplest cases, discovery favors the side with the deepest pockets. A large corporation employing a corporate law firm on an hourly basis can overwhelm the solo practitioner or small firm with expenses and discovery requests that exhaust the lawyer's and client's time and money, long before the case is ready for trial.

You can save an immense amount of time by asking directly for what you need and giving what you are supposed to give. Don't fight useless battles, and don't do unnecessary work.

Case in point: Lawyer A, doubtless billing his client by the hour, writes Lawyer B a 6-page letter on scheduling an upcoming deposition. Lawyer B writes Lawyer A: "The 26th at 10:00 PM is OK for the deposition."

If it looks as though discovery is going to be long, complex and expensive, you should seriously consider associating an attorney or firm that has the resources to share, or even to assume, the burden of discovery and trial. You may have to give up control over the case and more than half the fee under such an arrangement, but it may be the only way you can save the case (and your sanity).

Associating more experienced counsel with deeper pockets

is nothing to be embarrassed or feel bad about. Solo practitioners do it regularly. There is only so much that a lawyer and secretary can do in a day's time. In fact, working with an experienced lawyer is also a great and economical opportunity to learn.

Chapter Two

Preparing For Discovery

What is the case all about?—The Deep Issue

That means "What is this case *really* about?" You are not look-ing for a law-school answer about the elements of the cause of action—at least not at this point.

Ask yourself why this dispute is being litigated in the first place. If you are representing the plaintiff, it is essential that you know why your client feels that he is compelled to seek the aid of a lawyer and, if necessary, file a lawsuit and even proceed to trial. What is it it that keeps him from shrugging it off and getting on with his life? On the other hand, what keeps the defendant from settling?

If you represent the defendant, ask yourself and your client the same questions. Often the answer is straightforward and obvious: your client has been badly injured by the defendant's negligence in a traffic accident. The defendant's insurance com-pany believes that it will cost less to litigate than to settle.

In more personal cases, such as divorce and custody, it may take you quite a while to root out the deep issue.

This does not negate the iron rule that you must first and foremost plead the cause of action in a way that gets you past a motion to dismiss or summary judgment. You must plead and prove the facts supporting each element of your case to the trier of fact—judge or jury—to justify the result you are seeking. You must satisfy the requirements of black-letter law.

Yet the deep issue, the dispute that brings a case to court, is the one that will make or break your case.

I once represented a man against his ex-wife in an action she brought to terminate his visitation with his twelve-year-old daughter. The daughter testified to a number of sexually suggestive actions of my client during visitation, of which there were no witnesses or other corroborating evidence. I was able to demonstrate on cross-examination, however, that the custodial mother, who had taken the daughter with her when she moved to a distant state, intensely hated my client and had done everything in her power to turn daughter against father. This evidence profoundly affected the judge, and after hearing all the evidence, he ruled that my client had done nothing to require a change in visitation and further scolded the mother for attempting to alienate daughter from father.

By determining the deep issue in advance, I was able on cross-examination to turn the attention of the judge away from the actions of my client—which were innocuous but ill-advised—to the hatred of the ex-wife, and how it explained the testimony of the daughter. Once the judge accepted my framing of the issues (emphasizing the ex-wife's hostility), he went out of his way to justify his decision by mentioning that the daughter's testimony sounded as though she was parroting the lessons she had learned in school about recognizing sexual abuse.

Determine the deep issue or issues in a case as you began. Your client may not tell you; it may be too embarrassing. It might sink his case. It might put him in a bad light before the judge or jury. It might even be incriminating. If something smells fishy, keep digging. Law offices are magnets for all manner of cranks, sociopaths and otherwise dysfunctional characters. If the potential client has been to several lawyers before you and all of them declined to take him on as a client, you should be particularly suspicious. The time to evaluate your client is up front, not after you have spent hundreds of hours (and buckets of money) developing your case, only to realize that you have nothing to go on. Despite your best efforts, you will occasionally be taken in by someone who gets under your skin. When a case falls down around your ears, you will invariably recall the warning signs that you ignored or rationalized early on.

It's easier to withdraw from a case earlier than later, especially if you are being paid on a contingency basis. It's easier to deal with unfavorable facts up front that to discover them on the eve of trial, or, even worse, during the cross-examination of your client. This last admonishment is the result of bitter experience, and it will happen sooner or later to every lawyer who litigates. Cross-examine your client before opposing counsel does, and save yourself great sorrow.

I once was called in on three days notice to assist in a trial. The client had been sued by an insurance company for civil arson after his house burned down and his wife, an innocent party, had been paid the insurance proceeds. In spite of our best efforts, we lost. I later learned that our client's nickname was "The Torch."

In any event, you will learn whether or not you have a problem client shortly after discovery begins, because a problem client will resist producing unfavorable discovery.

You must prove two cases

It follows from the foregoing discussion that every case you litigate will require you to prove two related cases:

1. The factual, black letter, objective case that law school taught you to analyze; and,
2. The deep, psychological case. This is the case that will convince the trier of fact that a fair and just outcome requires that your client win. If you win the psychological battle, the trier of fact will view the evidence in your favor. In fact, if you successfully frame the psychological battle the trier of fact will often ignore evidence to the contrary. That's how human minds work. We decide who has been harmed and who caused the harm. Then we view the evidence (often unconsciously) in the light of the decision we have already made.

The "deep" case is the psychological one.

This does not mean, however, that facts don't matter. That large verdict you won by appealing to raw emotion in spite of the facts will often be set aside by the trial judge in a more rational moment, or even reversed on appeal. The cold transcript pages will fail to arouse anger or pity in the appellate ivory tower.

In order to ultimately prevail, you must win both factual and psychological cases.

I once was involved in a federal lawsuit by four mobile home dealers against one of the largest financial institutions in the world, which was defended by the largest law firm in the world. The documentary evidence filled several pickup trucks. It consisted almost totally of columns of numbers, representing the many sales of mobile homes that the bank had financed. The black-letter case was a long, technical, eye-glazing, mind-numbing, and posterior-abusing combination of industry practices, collections and the UCC. The principal legal issue was the duty of the holder of a recourse note to make reasonable efforts to collect payments from the maker of the note that financed his purchase of a mobile home.

The human issue was whether or not the mobile home dealers were treated fairly by a large, international bank. Our position was that the bank, after financing thousands of mobile home sales, literally shut down its customary collection practices, allowed the payments to become delinquent, foreclosed on the mobile homes, and then sold them for distressed values at auction a short distance from our clients' places of business. Then the bank demanded the deficiencies from our clients on the basis that the notes were transferred to them with recourse. We contended that the bank, by ceasing its customary method of collection, had quit using reasonable methods of collection and therefore could not avail themselves of recourse against the dealers, who were our clients. Further, we contended that the behavior the bank was deliberate and outrageous that the bank had deliberately driven our clients out of business.

Our black-letter case was not the strongest case we could have wished for, but our psychological case was very, very powerful. The bank's counsel did not help his client either, when he reminded the jury that he was a member of the world's biggest law firm and his client the world's biggest bank.

The jury returned a verdict larger than we had asked. Obviously, they were overwhelmed by the deep case. I suspect that they never really troubled themselves with the black-letter law or the elaborate printouts.

Chapter Three

Black-letter Law

Use Jury instructions

If your case is one that is normally tried before a jury, most states and Federal circuits publish or have readily available pattern jury instructions that cover virtually every type of case you will encounter. You can also purchase books of jury instructions from national publishers and local firms that specialize in particular jurisdictions. The elements of your cause of action, set out clearly and succinctly in the applicable instructions, should form a checklist for your complaint. You did consult the applicable jury instructions when you drafted the complaint, didn't you? If you didn't, do it now and hope that you did not leave something out. You would be surprised at the number of experienced attorneys who haven't learned this technique. Many of them can draft a perfect complaint by virtue of their experience and careful research into the law. You, on the other hand, can craft a near-perfect complaint merely by paraphrasing the applicable instruction, and you can probably do so more quickly.

The pattern instructions provided by the federal courts usually apply to peculiarly federal matters, such as civil rights, patent infringement, RICO, Americans With Disabilities Act

(ADA), discrimination in employment, Jones Act, etc. In diversity cases, you should use pattern instructions based on the applicable substantive state law and federal instructions that involve federal procedure. Look on the websites of the United States Courts of Appeals for federal instructions.

If you are defending, the jury instructions will also tell you what the plaintiff must prove to win and what remedies the jury may award. The instructions therefore present you with a list of targets for you to take aim at. If there are five essential elements in a cause of action, the defendant need only disprove one of them to win. The plaintiff must prove them all.

Use Statutes and Case Law for Authority

Unfortunately, there are numerous types of cases that are almost always tried before a judge, so pattern jury instructions will be unavailable. One does not instruct a judge the way the judge instructs a jury.

In such situations, you will usually find that either the legislature or the state's highest court has created the equivalent of instructions in statutes or reported opinions. For instance, in my state of Mississippi, the state supreme court, in *Allbright v. Allbright*, 437 So. 2d 1003, 1005 (Miss. 1983), set down eleven factors that trial courts must use in determining custody of minors and infants. The case is cited frequently during trials and forms the basis of the courts' opinions and judgements granting custody. You may not need to specifically plead all of the factors in your complaint, but you must deal with them in trial. When you appeal a custody judgment, you must argue the *Allbright* factors before the appellate courts.

So the rule here is to determine the controlling statutes or cases and treat them as jury instructions. There are treatises in most states on the various areas of practice in that state, and you are advised to consult them for authorities. In many cases, the treatises have become so familiar that they are cited as authorities themselves.

Research the Defenses

There is no point in proving all the elements of your claim if the defendant can successfully assert a valid defense. Sometimes jury instructions will include defenses along with the main elements. In other cases the defenses will be set out in a separate instruction. The same is true of matters that are usually tried before a judge. In any case, you must research the defenses in the cases, treatises and statutes.

Be Creative

While drawing up your complaint, the pleading that embodies your theory of the case, don't be too hasty.

Turn over the facts in your mind and try to imagine every possible cause of action and theory of the case, and put all of the non-frivolous ones in your complaint. Many important judicial decisions have stemmed from creative pleadings that convinced a court that it ought to change or extend a legal theory in order to arrive at a just result. Imagine that you are arguing your facts to an eight year-old child, a street person, a Chinese billionaire, a fireman, a yoga teacher, or a convict on death row. What you are trying to do is to gain different perspectives on your case. David Allen, the task management guru, once remarked that perspective is the single most valuable commodity in the world. Try to look at the facts of your case from as many viewpoints as possible in order to obtain a more comprehensive perspective of what your case is all about.

Undergoing these mental exercises will deepen your discovery requests and produce multiple possibilities on appeal if you are the appellant or the cross-appellant.

In the end, the judge and jury (and possibly the appellate court) will want to know "Just what this case is all about." You will need to have an answer that makes sense and fits the facts. Come up with as many narratives as possible that fit the facts and pick the most believable one that favors your client.

A good example of creative pleading is adding to a defamation claim a claim for invasion of privacy. Many states now recognize the tort of invasion of privacy (including holding the plaintiff in a "false light") which may be easier to prove than traditional common-law slander and libel.

Along with another solo lawyer, I once represented a dealer in industrial cleaners, whose business was nearly destroyed by a newspaper columnist's failure to understand how one of his chemicals was to be used. We filed a complaint sounding in 1) common-law libel and 2) invasion of privacy by holding the plaintiff in a false light. On the defendant's motion for summary judgment the court dismissed the libel counts but retained the invasion of privacy count. The newspaper settled shortly thereafter for a reasonable amount. Creative pleading won the case against some brilliant lawyers at a prestigious law firm.

Determine the relevant documents

- List the elements of your cause of action;
- Element by element, list the facts you will use to prove each;

- Next to the facts, list the documents and things you already know you will need to prove them.

In many cases you will not know the names of specific documents but can list them by categories, i.e., bank statements, cancelled checks, complaints received, and the like. I like to use a spreadsheet application on my computer to do this, since I can create as many columns and rows as I need. Outlining software that adds extra columns as needed can be useful at this stage.

Don't hesitate to ask advice of friends and colleagues that may be familiar with the subject matter. Frequently, acquaintances who work in relevant fields help me pinpoint exactly what I need to prove my cases.

- Beside the name of each document or thing, list the current owner or custodian, if known.

Sometimes you will know precisely what is relevant. In a medical malpractice case, the relevant documents consist of all your client's medical records, including X-rays, CAT scans, lab tests, etc, for each clinic, hospital, doctor and any other medical entity or person that treated your client. You will need expert testimony to prove the standard of care, that the defendant's actions or omissions violated the standard of care and that the injuries to the plaintiff were proximately caused by the violation by the defendant of that standard. You will need itemized costs of all treatments, especially the ones that your medical expert believes were necessitated by the alleged medical negligence of the defendant.

Other times, you will be going on a fishing expedition, for instance, looking for inculpatory email messages, evidence of previous negligent acts, previous lawsuits, etc. The only limit is time and money (yours or your client's) and the requirement that your requests be relevant to the subject matter of the case, or, in some jurisdictions, relevant to the issues raised in the pleadings.

Be aware of state and federal limitations on the scope of discovery, because the rules occasionally change, usually in the direction of narrowing the scope and amount of discovery. Initially there were no limitations on the number of interrogatories a party could propound to another party in the federal courts, but once solo practitioners and small firms acquired inexpensive word processors and were able to crank out the long, detailed requests that had previously been the prerogative of large law firms, the federal courts suddenly became concerned with the abuse of interrogatories and limited them to twenty-five. FRCP 26(b)(1) originally allowed the discovery of anything relevant to the subject matter of the case; since 2000 it allows the discovery of anything relevant to "any party's claim or defense."

Determine who has knowledge of facts

List all the persons you believe have knowledge of the facts of your case. When you do not know the individuals, list the category, being as specific as possible, i.e. policeman on duty at intersection of Sycamore and 1st Avenue, garbage truck driver, night-shift nurse on 2/1/2011, etc.

Next to each fact you must prove, write down the name of the person having knowledge of that fact and what you think she knows. Do not list only persons with favorable facts; you want an accurate portrait of your case, warts and all. Never forget that your object is to learn at least as much about your opponent's case as he knows and preferably more.

Your client may or may not be able to help with this, depending upon the circumstances. Usually, the client will know most of the people involved and what happened.

List what you can prove now

Now that you know precisely what you must prove (and disprove) and the evidence you need to do this, you can organize your discovery.

List the elements of your claim, or, if defending, your opponent's claim. Under each element list precisely the facts you can prove with what you now have and what or whom you will use to prove them. On the spreadsheet, simply add extra columns for this information.

If defending, list the facts the plaintiff must prove, how you know or think he is going to prove them, and any evidence you or your client now have to negate any of those elements.

Determine what defenses your opponents can prove now

You should list the elements of any possible defenses of your opponent (assuming you are the plaintiff), what he can prove now and what evidence you now have that would negate those defenses. Since you have already listed the defenses, it should be fairly obvious what documents and testimony (including expert testimony) the defendant will need to support his defense.

For instance, if you have filed an action for fraud, defenses will consist of anything that can negate any one of the elements of fraud, plus any affirmative defenses that as a matter of law constitute defenses to fraud.

Some affirmative defenses are a complete defense, such as when a defendant in a defamation action can show that she spoke the truth.

There are also statutory defenses, such as statutes of limitations.

As you learn of new evidence that supports your opponent's case, list it here under defenses.

Determine what to prove through your opponent or a 3d party

When you know which elements you can prove with the credible evidence you now have, what remains are the elements you must prove through either a third party or your opponent.

List documents & things from the opposing side & third parties

List the documents and things you will need. In the case of third parties, you may need to subpoena any documents you require, especially if they are financial or medical records. Sometimes a bit of diplomacy will get them. Some may be publicly available.

List witnesses you need to depose

A deposition is a recorded (and usually transcribed) examination of a witness under oath, usually taken prior to trial.

List deposition witnesses as friendly or hostile, with a brief summary of what you expect each deponent to say and the significance of the testimony in proving your case.

Remember that deposing a party or potential witness takes

time and money, so do not waste your resources when it is unlikely to make a difference. After studying the case, you may feel that it will not be necessary to depose every witness who knows something about the case, and you could possibly save yourself and your client money by not deposing them. Discuss this thoroughly with your client and confirm in a letter to your client that both of you have agreed not to depose certain witnesses.

When you decide not to depose a cooperative witness, have her sign an affidavit to keep her honest at trial. If you have satisfactory answers to an interrogatory or an admission from the other party, you may often dispense with a witness that would only repeat the answers. But don't forget the affidavit!

List facts for admission and denial

List facts that the other side might be willing to admit or deny under oath. As a general rule, you will not want an admission of a fact that will have a decisive impact on a jury. This would include any testimony that will arouse the emotions of the trier of fact in favor of your client. Once a fact is admitted or stipulated, the judge may not allow you to explore that fact in depth with a witness, and often the simple recitation of a bare fact before the jury barely sinks into their consciousness. It is hard to win the psychological case with bare, objective facts.

On the other hand, a party that refuses to admit a fact generally has to pay the expenses incurred by the requesting party in proving the fact.

Proving a scientific or technical fact can often be expensive, so it never hurts to request an admission in those cases. Highly technical testimony will seldom have an emotional impact on a jury, so if the parties can stipulate to technical or scientific facts, you could save substantial expert witness fees.

List factual questions for interrogatories

List factual questions for interrogatories that may require research or knowledge that you would not expect to be revealed in a deposition.

You will be using interrogatories to ascertain facts that may require research or take time answering by the opposite party. You will want to draw up your questions as broadly as possible (so that you don't miss relevant information) but not so broadly that you end up with too much information to comfortably handle or have to deal with an objection to the interrogatory on the grounds of over-broadness.

Go back over your list of the elements of your cause of action and the evidence supporting each one. Where are your weaknesses? This might be a good area for an interrogatory.

Chapter Four

Electronic Discovery

A spectre is haunting litigation practice—the spectre of electronic discovery.

It was inevitable, of course. As firms and individuals have increasingly conducted their business with computers and connected them to the internet, vital evidence has accumulated on floppy disks, hard disks, magnetic tapes, flash drives, and optical media, as well as the "cloud"—remote servers scattered around the globe. Electronic evidence is often more important than paper in ascertaining the truth. It is likely that most of your future cases will involve discovery of electronically-stored evidence.

This book assumes that your client is not a firm with thousands of employees and terabytes of data. For large corporations, electronic discovery can cost literally millions of dollars in IT and legal fees, and such companies invariably retain large firms to do their legal work. Your client either owns a small business or her case is personal, such as a divorce or personal injury.

Electronic evidence has several characteristics that set it apart from written and printed documentation:

1. It is voluminous;
2. The media it resides upon will inevitably become corrupted in time and even when intact, may be irretrievable because no hardware to read it is still available. Eight-inch floppy disks are now subject to both these problems, especially since many of them were originally recorded in proprietary formats;
3. It can be analyzed by computers at high speed;
4. It is fragile because it is easy to modify; but,
5. It is also extremely persistent, because numerous copies often exist on different computers and servers. Every time an email is sent, at least two copies are created. As an email winds its way through the Internet from server to server, more copies are created.

For these reasons, The Federal Rules of Civil Procedure, in particular, Rules 26 and 34, have been amended to provide for electronic discovery. Here are the bare bones of what the rules require:

Instruct your client to preserve all relevant records

As soon as litigation is anticipated, your client must immediately cease destruction of records that are related or might be related to the subject matter of the lawsuit and take affirmative measures to preserve existing data. Your client is not in the position to split hairs at this time over whether or not a document is relevant. Everything must be saved. There are no exceptions to this requirement.

In the ideal scenario, as soon as a "trigger" occurs that lets you or your client know that litigation is in the offing, your client temporarily shuts down the office and calls in an IT technician to make a clone of every hard drive in the company on either new hard drives or DVDs. A less stringent—but almost equally effective—course would be to clone only the user directories of each hard drive, since the system files are unlikely to contain discoverable data.

Explain to your client that it is not difficult for an expert to determine whether or not electronic records have been erased and that the penalties for destruction of evidence are too awful to contemplate. Your client is responsible for insuring that his employees understand and comply with a do-not-destroy policy. If it turns out that discoverable evidence has been destroyed, at best the jury will be instructed to presume that the destroyed documents would have been unfavorable to your client's case; at worst, the court may enter judgment against your client and refer him to the U.S. Attorney for criminal prosecution on a charge of obstruction of justice.

If your client uses an online mail service like Yahoo! or Google Mail, he must produce all relevant messages, tedious though it might be, which is a good reason not to conduct business through an online service. Businesses should insist that employees send and receive all business-related email using the company email. Equally important is that they use company email exclusively for company business and use another service, like Google Mail or Yahoo! for personal correspondence.

You should discourage your client from using only backup applications designed merely to restore a crashed hard disk or a computer destroyed in a fire. Such applications usually take a snapshot of the hard disk in a proprietary format that is not designed for indexing and searching. To access such a backup—

usually a tape cartridge—often the entire hard disk must be restored from the tape before it can be indexed and searched, a process that is time-consuming and expensive. Using such a system as one of his backup components is okay.

Archiving must continue during the pendency of the litigation.

Most jurisdictions make a distinction between readily available records and older records that require great expense to produce. For the less accessible category, the court will normally not require you to produce the records, but if it does, the court will probably require your opponent to pay part or all of the costs of translating obsolete media into accessible form.

Ensure that your regular clients have reasonable backup and destruction policies and enforce them

Your job will be much easier if your client has a record retention and destruction policy that 1) is reasonable and 2) is followed consistently.

All business that use computers should ideally have a bullet-proof backup capability that preserves two copies of all documents, one of which is off-site.

No one, absent special statutory requirements, is required to maintain business records indefinitely, on the offhand chance that she might someday sue or be sued. Your client should destroy records that have no reason to be kept. This will vary from client to client, depending upon the nature of the business and whether the business is subject to a regulatory framework that mandates either retention or destruction of particular records.

Therefore, you should urge all your business clients to adopt and publish in writing to all their employees a document and file retention and destruction policy, and to ensure that it is followed, irrespective of whether litigation is in the offing or not. The keyword is "reasonable." The safe thing to do is to err by retaining too much, rather than too little. Keep in mind that a reasonable retention and destruction police that is inconsistently followed (or not followed at all) will probably not be considered reasonable by the judge, and your client will suffer for it.

Prepare for the initial discovery conference

FRCP 26(f) requires the parties to confer as soon as practicable about a number of items, including making arrangements for the preservation of evidence and formulating a discovery plan. It is here that you will have to let the other parties know what electronic material you are after and to disclose any issues you might have in complying with the electronic discovery requirements. The rule requires that matters of privilege be raised here as well as timing for initial disclosure. In short, the rule anticipates that the discovery plan will resolve all issues that can be resolved between the parties and sets out the issues that may have to be resolved by the court.

It is wise at this point to agree upon the type of media the parties will use to produce discovery material. CDs and DVDs are the usual media, but you may agree to use a cloud service like Dropbox, flash drives, or even old-fashioned printed copies. It all boils down to the convenience of the parties, but it's best to agree up front.

Caviat: due to the nature of the e-discovery process, there is a more than minimal likelihood that you may inadvertently disclose privileged material. You should insist on a "clawback" provision in the discovery plan that protects you from inadvertent waiver and requires the other side to return any accidentally-disclosed privileged material.

State rules regarding electronic discovery may differ. Most states do not require a discovery plan or an initial discovery conference, but all of them provide for reasonable discovery of electronic records. In the case of discovery disputes, state courts are likely to consult and adopt federal case law, given that it is so well-developed.

Use a professional on voluminous data

If your client's computers contain many gigabytes of email or other documents, and it is not clear how discoverable material can be separated from non-discoverable, hire an IT expert familiar with electronic discovery. There are numerous electronic discovery firms with powerful, highly specialized software that can comb through terabytes of data in a reasonable length of time and produce an indexed and filtered collection of relevant information, ready for review. The guy at the local computer store may be a computer genius, but he is unlikely to be an expert in electronic discovery. Call around and learn whom lawyers are using and with whom they are pleased. Even if you are a computer expert, your time will be better spent practicing law than worrying about technical minutiae. You will have your hands full reviewing the documents before turning them over to opposing counsel.

Negotiate for reasonable disclosure

Several years ago I represented two owners of a tax preparation company against a third owner in a fight over the dissolution of the business. An acrimonious dissolution is invariably a mess. Usually, the business owns fewer assets than are sufficient to pay the attorney fees. To make our case even more complicated, a local bank held a secured note on the assets of the company.

The bank's attorney submitted a request for all the email sent by the company for two years, which would have included tens of thousands of messages containing tax advice from the staff of the company to the clients. Beside the problem of confidentiality between tax preparers and their clients, we were faced with the problem of separating personal messages from the business ones.

Knowing that the bank was interested in protecting its collateral, I asked the clients to copy all the messages having to do with an offer to buy the company's trademark, its only asset. The collection amounted to about twenty messages. I produced those messages to the bank's attorney and objected to production of the rest as irrelevant. The bank's attorney was satisfied, and we avoided a considerable amount of expenses and time sifting through the entire corporate message file.

The rule here is ascertain what the other side really wants from electronic discovery. Make your best efforts to narrow the scope of electronic discovery, and then furnish the other side with what you have agreed on. Most of the time, opposing counsel will be thrilled with having to review a few hundred documents rather than a few hundred thousand. You will have avoided some hefty expenses that your client would otherwise have to pay.

Chapter Five

Order Of Discovery

Avoid educating the other side

You are not obligated to reveal to the other side how you plan to win your case. Most of the time, however, your strategy will be obvious, because countless plaintiffs and defendants have trod the same path before. On the other hand, every case is unique in at least one respect and often in several respects. You are obligated to respond to your opponents' discovery requests fully and in good faith, but you need go no further.

Interrogatories in particular can educate the opposite side, which is why you should serve the bulk of them only after you have received the documents you requested and deposed your opponent and key witnesses. See below for more about interrogatories.

Federal - initial disclosure under FRAP 26(a)

In Federal court, the parties have somewhat less flexibility in determining the course of discovery, since the discovery rules have been amended to require the disclosure of large categories of information and documents before the discovery period even begins. Most courts also enter discovery scheduling orders as a matter of course, often after a short meeting with the attorneys. They will usually allow more time for discovery in complex cases, so if you expect discovery to be long and contentious, you should inform the court at the outset, so that you will not be filing too many motions to amend the scheduling order. These requirements are also subject to local court rules that may tighten or relax the initial disclosure requirements. Familiarize yourself thoroughly with both before you file a civil action.

Keep in mind that Rule 26(a)(1)(E) provides that a party "must make its initial disclosures based on the information then reasonably available to it. A party is not excused from making its disclosures because it has not fully investigated the case or because it challenges the sufficiency of another party's disclosures or because another party has not made its disclosures." The keyword here is "reasonably," and it gives the judge or magistrate considerable discretion in determining whether you have complied with the initial disclosure requirements. This can be a problem when a piece of key evidence, such as an internal memo, is in the possession of a corporate defendant, but you don't yet know that it exists. A famous example of this is the exploding gas tank memo in the Ford Pinto case, which showed that Ford had long been aware of the fire hazard of an exposed rear gas tank.

The purpose of initial disclosure is to show to the opposing side (and ultimately the trial court) that you have enough evidence to overcome a motion to dismiss or to demonstrate a reasonable probability that, given sufficient discovery, you will acquire sufficient evidence. This can be unfair to a plaintiff whose case rests upon proving the intent of a corporate defendant, whose intent can often be proved only by extensive discovery. In federal court it is a hurdle that must be overcome, however.

The requirements for preliminary disclosure are very thorough. Since you have already (hopefully) researched your case in detail before filing it, your preliminary disclosures must include nearly everything you and your client possess or control that support your pleadings. If you have consulted an expert witness and expect him to testify, you must produce a signed report, even if your expert hasn't yet submitted one to you.

Remember, failing to make the required disclosures in a timely way can lead to heartburn and heartbreak, including monetary sanctions, exclusion of your evidence at trial, or even summary judgment or dismissal. If, given the probable return on your (or your client's) investment of money and time, you feel that the discovery process for a case is too onerous or expensive, tell your client to find another lawyer. Get out of the case early, before you file your complaint and became irresistibly drawn into the discovery vortex.

Ask for documents and things first

In most cases, the documentary evidence determines who will win.

Look carefully at the list of documents and other things you believe that the other side possesses and generalize each of these categories to create a request that cannot be evaded simply by being taken literally.

For instance, if you think that the defendant wrote a check to a third party sometime in March 2007, you could phrase your request, "Produce all checks written by defendant to John Q. Jones in March 2007," or you could phrase it this way: "Produce all cancelled checks, check registers, bank statements, and deposit slips for all bank accounts for which the defendant is a signatory, beneficiary, or over which the defendant exercises any level of control, for the period January 1, 2007 to June 30, 2007."

The advantage of this request over the first one is that it does not reveal the specific check, payee or date of the check you are looking for. It also provides for the contingency that the check you are looking for might have been written on February 28 or April 1, in which case the first request would have not required the other side to produce it.

Of course, you must use common sense. You would obviously not submit the second request to General Motors or IBM. Depending on the size of the defendant, a court might regard the request as too broad. Reasonability is the touchstone of discovery practice, and it applies particularly to the scope and breadth of discovery requests. Make your interrogatories reasonable but prepare to defend their reasonableness against an objection based on over-broadness.

Since interrogatories have been limited in number in many courts, the courts are apt to interpret interrogatories broadly and to look dimly upon hair-splitting objections.

The two- or three-page list of "definitions" with which many lawyers preface their discovery requests have little value. A lawyer from a large firm once confessed to me that he and his partners included the list of definitions solely for the purpose of impressing their corporate clients.

Instead of beginning your interrogatories with three pages of definitions, insert something like the following sentence at the beginning of your requests: "These [requests|interrogatories] are to be interpreted and the terms therein are to be defined as broadly as possible in keeping with the purpose of the [name of procedural rules]."

Who pays for copies and other expenses of discovery?

Usually, each party pays for the cost of responding to discovery.

Most of the time, the cost of copying documents and electronic media is small enough that it's not worth haggling over. By absorbing your own costs, you also keep your original documents in-house and out of the hands of opposing counsel.

If the response is voluminous, however, scanning the documents, as opposed to making copies, will save your client quite a bit of cost and will furnish you with electronic copies at no extra expense to your client.

If the opposing party's discovery requests are oppressive, however, you should demand that the cost be shared, and be prepared to ask the court for relief if the parties cannot agree to split the cost.

What form should your responses take?

Most of the time, opposing counsel will be happy to receive scanned images saved on a CD or DVD in easily readable form, such as PDF files. Email can be produced as text files. If there are just a few documents, it is probably easier to photocopy them and send them by regular mail.

If your client's records are organized, you must furnish them to opposing counsel with substantially the same organization. If they are in a proprietary computer format not easily accessible to opposing counsel, FRCP 34 requires that your client have it translated into usable form. This is less of a problem today that it was in the early days of personal computers, since .doc and .docx (Word), .pdf (Acrobat) and .xlr (Excel) files are almost universally readable and most software used today is capable of exporting internal data in those formats.

Hint: Word and Excel files can be easily modified, either intentionally or accidentally. If the formulas contained in the files are not at issue, produce the files in locked Acrobat format (.pdf) and the recipient will not be able to modify the contents easily. On a Mac, there is an option to print directly to .pdf. On most Windows PCs, you will probably need to purchase an inexpensive or free program like PDF Creator.

When in doubt about the form of your response, ask opposing counsel. Most lawyers will be happy to receive discovery in a form that doesn't take up much storage and is easy to review.

Preparing to depose the opposite party

You generally have three objectives in deposing a witness:

1. To find out what the witness knows about the case and is willing to testify to under oath;

2. To find out whether additional relevant documents exist and whether there are additional witnesses that have relevant knowledge; and,

3. To lock in the witness's testimony so the he or she will not change her testimony before or during trial. This includes your own witnesses as well as witnesses from the other side. Sometimes your own witnesses will change their testimony at trial to avoid embarrassment or to keep from offending friends or family members, or for darker reasons, such as subtle pressure by colleagues or employ-

ers, or even for bribes. When big money is at stake, it is best to take no chances.

A fourth possible objective is to catch an opposing witness in a lie, in which case you can discredit the witness during trial, no matter how he testifies. If he attempts to tell the truth, you have the sworn deposition with which to impeach him. If he persists in the lie, you can expose his falsehood.

Think deeply about the purpose of the deposition and each question. It is wise to write down your questions verbatim in advance. That way, you can be reasonably sure that you will have covered what you planned and can annotate a question if you need followup. At the minimum, prepare a thorough outline of what you need to cover. It will not only keep you on track, it will impress opposing counsel with your diligence and let them know that you are not a pushover. That will put pressure on the opposing party to settle.

In addition, writing your deposition questions will stimulate your brain to generate additional questions and paths of inquiry that you would not have thought of otherwise. There is a kind of magic in putting your thoughts to paper that activates the creative faculties.

Consultant and self-management writer David Allen makes the point that when one has the energy to do a task, one usually doesn't have the energy to think about what one ought to be doing; when the time for action arrives, the thinking should have already been done. Think of yourself as a musician preparing to perform a difficult classical composition before an audience; as little as possible should be left to chance. The reason for writing out your questions in advance is that you don't want to be composing your next question in your mind while you are listening to the deponent answer the question you just asked. You should be concentrating one hundred percent on what the deponent is saying, because otherwise you will miss many opportunities to explore highly relevant areas that you previously did not suspect. You can then safely digress, thoroughly explore the unexpected areas, and then return to your planned questions without losing your original thread. Keep in mind, however, that a single answer may change the entire case and render the remainder of your questions irrelevant. Listen carefully and be prepared to turn on a dime when circumstances require.

To determine in advance what questions you should ask, go back to your table of issues and see what you need to prove. You should cover all the areas in which you reasonably believe the deponent might have knowledge. Some of your questions will be fishing and should be broad, so as to catch items that might seem unimportant to the deponent but which are actually material and relevant. A typical fishing question would be "Have you ever visited Jacksonville?" rather than "Were you in Jacksonville on April 28, 2005?"

Alternatively, you may need to elicit testimony that the deponent would prefer not to answer, in which case, your question must be phrased to pin her down with no wiggle room. Example: "On April 28, 2005 around ten o'clock in the morning, were you standing on the sidewalk of Kings Road in front of the Jacksonville, Florida main post office?"

Since it is impossible for you to know in advance all the answers that will be forthcoming, list alternate questions in advance and then choose the most appropriate question depending upon previous answers. This allows you to adjust to whatever answer the deponent gives to a particular question.

The deponent must answer all your questions unless they are irrelevant or call for privileged information. Attorneys frequently object to the form of the question, but the deponent must answer it. If the question calls for privileged information, the opposing counsel will object and instruct the witness not to answer. If it is your question, you should ask opposing counsel on the record exactly why the information is privileged. If you do not believe his answer to be meritorious, you can file a motion to compel and the transcript of the deposition will serve as your evidence. Whether or not you should go to the trouble depends on the strength of your argument and the importance to your case of the withheld testimony.

The rule is to never waste time and energy on peripheral issues. Your job is to win the case, not an argument.

Preparing your witnesses for deposition

Do not expect your non-expert witnesses to know anything at all about depositions. You must prepare them by explaining in detail:

1. What a deposition is about, including its scope and purpose;
2. What you expect from the witness in the way of manners, demeanor, and responses to the questions from the other side;
3. How the witness is to respond when an attorney makes an objection;
4. You must explain that the witness must tell the truth but

should not try to be helpful or to guess the answer. Many deponents go into a deposition as though it were an examination before a teacher or professor, and feel that their job is to please the attorney who will be deposing them. Disabuse them of that misconception. Tell them that this is a lawsuit and pleasing opposing counsel is the very last thing they should strive to do.

You must then—in fine detail—cover the subject matter of the deposition with the witness by asking him every question that you anticipate might be asked by opposing counsel, ensuring as much as possible that the witness will not be blindsided or surprised.

Appendix A of this book contains a highly-regarded set of instructions for deposition witnesses that you may reproduce and give to your deponents to prepare themselves.

Depositions to preserve testimony

Quite often, you will require the testimony of a witness who, because of reasons of health, expense, or inconvenience, cannot attend trial. Use a deposition to perpetuate his testimony.

When you serve notice of the deposition, state in your notice that the purpose of the deposition is to preserve testimony and may be used in trial in lieu of live testimony.

This is a good time to conduct a video deposition, especially if the witness is attractive and testifies convincingly. As an alternative, you may have the transcript of the deposition read in court by virtually anyone you choose.

There are some very good reasons to take a video deposition. It captures the facial expressions, the tone of voice, the body language, and all the other nonverbal messages that people send out as a part of being human. By reviewing the tape or file you can gain some useful clues about the state of the mind of the deponent at the time she is answering questions.

For many people, being recorded on video is an intimidating experience. The average person has never given a deposition and his apprehensiveness is normally magnified by the presence of a video camera.

I was once involved in a 29 USC §1983 lawsuit against a local college that had fired a professor for what I believe were highly illegal reasons. My first discovery request was for video depositions of the president and the academic dean of the college, which they resisted to the point of filing for a protective order in the District Court. Their motion was quickly overruled and I took both depositions in the offices of their counsel. The president acted at such a low-functioning level during the deposition that I believe he was under the influence of tranquilizers or anti-anxiety medicine. The academic dean, a woman, was extremely hostile and evasive. Their feigned ignorance was so transparent that any jury would have seen through it in a second.

It was not long after those two depositions that the college offered a fair settlement and my client accepted. Interestingly, the college insisted, as one of the conditions of settlement, that the tapes of the depositions remain confidential and not be released to any third party.

So do not hesitate to schedule video or audio depositions, even if, as in our jurisdiction, the federal judges have created unreasonable expenses. There will be times when the cost is worth it.

Opposing counsel may object during the deposition and may also object in writing to certain parts of the deposition on the usual evidentiary grounds. The court will then view the video or transcript and rule on the objections as though the witness were testifying at trial. If the court sustains objections to certain parts of the testimony, they can be redacted from the transcript before it is read or edited out of the video version before being shown to the jury.

During the videotaping of a deposition, you will occasionally encounter an opposing counsel who frequently interrupts your witness and interposes numerous objections in an attempt to render the video version useless. Do not let this happen. If you find yourself in this situation, it is best to call out the the offending attorney on his behavior while the video recorder is still running and admonish him to wait until the witness is finished before he makes an objection. If he persists, stop the deposition and immediately file a motion for protective order requesting sanctions, especially if you have incurred significant expenses, such as an expert's fee. You will have on video all the evidence you need in support of your motion.

Deposition mechanics

If you wish to take the deposition of a witness, the first step is calling the opposing attorney and scheduling a date, time and location at which the deposition will be held. He will telephone his client and the witness if it happens to be one of his and then call you back with open dates. The two of you will then agree on a date, time, and location, after which you must immediately mail him a Notice of Deposition, setting out date, time and location, the type of deposition and the means by which it will be recorded or otherwise memorialized.

The deposition can take place at any location upon which you agree. If you have a home office, taking a deposition in your home is not a practical course, so suggest that you conduct the deposition in opposing counsel's office, particularly if opposing counsel works for a large law firm. There is no end to the number of possible locations. I have used conference rooms in libraries, businesses, courthouses, and even storerooms.

If it is your deposition, you have the choice – within the rules of your jurisdiction – to choose a court reporter or other means of recording the deposition. If you choose to use a court reporter, you must call the court reporter or court reporting agency and schedule the court reporter. There will be an appearance fee and then a fee per page. If this is a really critical deposition, it is probably wise to use a court reporter.

Some jurisdictions allow you to record a deposition by video or audio recorder without the necessity and expense of a court reporter. Since the cost of court reporters can be burdensome, especially if there are numerous deponents and you are handling a case on a contingency basis, you should ascertain the bare-bones requirement for memorializing the deposition. In my federal jurisdiction, the court adopted local rules requiring a court reporter at all depositions, irrespective of whether the deposition was recorded, either in audio or video. A few years later, the court added an additional expense by requiring for an audio or video deposition that a qualified technician record and certify the recording as to accuracy and authenticity. Since the requirement of a court reporter remained unchanged, and thus the accuracy of a recording could be easily checked by comparing it with the transcript, it is difficult to conclude anything other than the court simply wanted to raise the expense and complexity of recording a deposition. Hopefully, the local and federal judges in your jurisdiction will not be so inclined.

In contrast, the state courts in my jurisdiction allow depositions to be recorded with a video camera on a tripod without a court reporter, simply by noticing the video deposition in the usual manner. The deposing lawyer sets up the camera and tripod, and the deponent is seated at the end of a long table, with opposing counsel on each side. The deponent is sworn on camera by a notary public.

The video camera provides a timestamp accurate to the second and the resulting video cassette or DVD can be reproduced and distributed to all counsel at minimal expense. If necessary, the deposition, or parts thereof, can be transcribed by any typist if the parties agree, but most of the time transcription is not necessary, especially as most cases settle before trial.

If you plan to memorialize the deposition by any means other than a court reporter, it is important to state in the notice of deposition the method by which the deposition will be recorded. Opposing counsel may opt to hire a court reporter if you are doing a video-only deposition.

It is a good idea to call opposing counsel a day or two in advance to confirm that the deposition will take place. In the legal world, there are many contingencies, and occasionally a change in schedule slips between the cracks, and you will not be notified. Witnesses can become sick, lawyers can be suddenly called out-of-town, and a thousand other mishaps can happen that will necessitate the continuance of the deposition.

Early in my practice, I was representing a client seeking to have a will declared invalid because of undue influence. In the course of representing this client, I scheduled a deposition of the proponent of the will, to be held in the office of her counsel. Unfortunately, I neglected to write it down, so on the day of the deposition I was surprised and horrified when I received a call from opposing counsel inquiring why I was absent for the deposition. To make it worse, I had neglected to schedule a court reporter. I was extremely lucky in that I had recently written two appeals to the state supreme court involving undue influence, so I was familiar with the statutory and case law dealing with undue influence. Consequently, although I had not reviewed the file and familiarized myself with the facts of the case, I knew precisely what I needed to prove undue influence upon the testatrix.

I hastened to opposing counsel's office, equipped with a small cassette recording machine, which I could use under the state Rules of Civil Procedure. Not only did I depose of the proponent of the will, I had also noticed opposing counsel, who had been involved in drafting the will, so I deposed him, also. As you can imagine, those were very intense depositions for me. Later, my secretary transcribed the tape of the depositions and both parties agreed that they were accurate.

Lesson learned: it is possible to conduct a deposition off-the-cuff, but the result is never as good as when you are well-prepared. While my questioning of the deponents was passable, and occasionally excellent, there were some minor facts I missed that would have made the case a lot easier to litigate. There were some questions I failed to ask that might have been devastating to the other side. Sometimes a well-prepared series of question in a deposition may prompt an on-the-spot offer of settlement.

Conducting a Deposition

Depositions are usually conducted at rectangular conference tables. The court reporter will sit at one end of the table, and the witness will sit next to the court reporter. Occasionally, the witness will sit at the end of the table, and the court reporter will sit slightly behind the witness to her right or left. You will sit across the table from or next to the witness because you will be interrogating the witness and handing her documents. Opposing counsel will sit across the table from you. Any assistants or other associates will sit on the appropriate side further away from the deponent.

The court reporter will need to know everyone's name who is attending. You can give her your card or simply speak it out loud. She will also probably want to know if this is a rush job and who wants copies of the deposition transcript. If you are paying the court reporter fees, you are usually entitled to an extra copy, but if not, you can always copy the original of transcript. If you purchase a transcript, you are usually provided an electronic copy which you may use for searching purposes.

After the preliminary matters are taken care of, you will then go on the record, and the reporter will start transcribing whatever is said. It is a good idea to reiterate the usual rules involving objections. Normally, objections are reserved until such time as a party offers the material into evidence or attempts to use it in some other manner. The exceptions are 1. Objections as to the form of the question and 2. Matters of privilege. When an objection is made as to the form of the question, the witness must answer the question as best she can. A witness does not have to answer questions that require privileged information for their answer. Under those circumstances, the attorney should not only object to the question as calling for privileged information, but also should instruct her witness not to answer the question. If you have asked a question that you believe does not call for privileged material, and opposing counsel instructs her client not to answer the question on the grounds of privilege, you have several options. You may either stop asking questions, announce that the deposition will be continued to a later date, and file a motion to compel, or you may continue asking questions and file such a motion afterwards. If the information is not critical to your case, the best course is to let it drop and keep going. On the other hand, if opposing counsel is particularly anxious that the information not be elicited from his client, then it might be wiser to ask the court's assistance, on the offhand chance that the witness and his counsel know something that they really don't want you to know. The testimony withheld may be merely embarrassing to the witness, but on the other hand, it might be devastating to her case.

If this is your deposition, opposing counsel may or may not want to ask questions of the witness. If he does, then you have the opportunity to ask question on redirect examination to clarify any answers opposing counsel has elicited.

Once the deposition is over, shake hands and leave. Do not hang around or socialize with opposing counsel.

Interrogatories

Even though it is a better practice to serve interrogatories on the opposite party after depositions, in the absence of initial disclosure requirements you will need the name of any expert witnesses your opponent plans to introduce, his professional qualifications, and what he or she will testify to in court as soon as possible. You will need this information for two purposes: 1) you need to know whether or not to hire your own expert and what his field should be, and 2) after consulting with your own expert, you will need to depose your opponent's expert.

You will also want to know the names and addresses of persons having knowledge of any facts relevant to the case and whom your opponent plans to call as a witness at trial. If you know what types of documentary evidence you will need, you should ask the opposing side the location of the documents and the name of the custodian. This could be important if your opponent does not possess or control access to the documents but knows who has them.

The rule here is—in the absence of a requirement of preliminary disclosure—get the documents and things and the answers to the above interrogatories first, find the appropriate expert (if you do not already have one), give her the facts and the reports of the opposing side's expert witness, and then ask her to educate you on the application of the science to the facts of your case. Then, having been thoroughly prepared by your expert as to the relevant scientific or other specialized issues, depose your opponent's expert.

It is advantageous for your expert to be present when you are deposing your opponent's expert. This may not be automatically allowed in some jurisdictions, but you can agree with opposing counsel to have each party's expert present when the other party's expert is being examined.

Once again, I remind you to ascertain in advance the "deep"

issue. This is particularly true in cases that rest on scientific opinion, where the complexity of the subject can easily obscure what you must prove, both from a legal and a psychological standpoint. You want the trier of fact to strongly believe—as well as intellectually understand—that your client should win.

So take out your list of what has to be proved (or disproved) to win your case. By the time you have received what your opponent has told you are all the relevant documents and deposed the other parties and relevant witnesses, including experts, you should be able to check off almost all the elements that you need to prove both your cases. If there are any remaining holes in your case, or you feel that evidence proving one or more elements of your case is a bit thin, you may want to draft some specific interrogatories aimed at those elements. This goes for the psychological proof as well as the objective proof.

When to use subpoenas

When you need materials for your case that are in the possession or control of a third party, then you must subpoena the materials. Depending on the kind of materials and the relationship of the third party to your opposing party, you may be able to obtain the materials simply by asking. Yet always give yourself ample time before the applicable deadlines to issue a subpoena and to enforce it in court, if necessary. Most third parties do not want to be drawn into a lawsuit, and you may have to force them by subpoena or even threat of a citation for contempt to furnish evidence or give testimony.

The same goes for depositions. With parties, a simple notice is the only requirement. To depose a non-party, you must serve them with a subpoena.

Always contact opposing counsel first to agree on deposition dates (including alternate dates); then contact the third party you wish to depose and arrange for the date, time and place. Then serve the deponent with a subpoena. Of course, if the deponent is hostile or makes himself scarce, simply serve him with a subpoena and negotiate dates, times and places afterwards.

Summary

The key to the mechanics of discovery is reasonableness. Most attorneys are reasonable and will ask in discovery only for what they need. Most attorneys will respond to discovery requests reasonably and promptly. In game theory, the most likely strategy for winners is always to treat the other side fairly and reasonably the first time and then to respond in kind after that. Be familiar with the rules and follow them so that you can advance your case.

Chapter Six

Approaches To Responding
To Discovery Requests

Generally

You must respond in writing to a discovery request in a timely way. You risk waiving your objections to the requests (including requests for privileged material) if you fail to respond in time. If you are unable to respond on time, contact opposing counsel and ask for more time. He will ordinarily consent, expecting a similar favor on a future occasion. Draft a joint order to be signed by all counsel extending the discovery period and have the judge sign it. If opposing counsel does not agree, you will have to file a motion for an enlargement of time with the court. The judge will expect to hear a specific reason for the enlargement, not an excuse of general busyness.

Timely responses will surprise and impress opposing counsel, which increases your standing. It will let opposing counsel know that you are serious and that he will have to work hard to have a chance of winning. The value of your settlement will go up.

You must respond to your opponent's discovery requests with whatever your client possesses or controls that responds to the request, is relevant to the case, and is not privileged. Any discoverable fact or evidence in your or your client's possession or control must be turned over if requested, or you will not be able to offer it into evidence at trial. If you acquire new evidence or learn new discoverable facts after responding, you must usually supplement your previous responses.

The bare minimum

There are three approaches to responding to discovery. Some lawyers believe that you should respond with the bare minimum necessary to satisfy the rules. Others like to overwhelm their opponents with voluminous discovery to keep their opponents busy and to cost them money. The third group approach is to assemble sufficient materials to impress the other side with the merits of your case.

The first group, the minimalists, prefer to err on the side of furnishing too little information in response, rather than too much. The reasoning is that there is no point in turning over anything that may hurt your own case, unless required. The problem with this approach in the federal system is that FRCP 26 requires as a part of preliminary disclosure "a copy—or a description by category and location—of all documents, electronically stored information, and tangible things that the disclosing party has in its possession, custody, or control and may use to support its claims or defenses, unless the use would be solely for impeachment." This means, in essence, that you must turn over to the other side the evidence with which you intend to prove your black-letter case before discovery even starts.

If you have evidence unfavorable to your side, however, you are not required to furnish it to the other side as a part of your preliminary disclosure, since it is unlikely that you will be using it to support your side's "claims or defenses," and there is always the possibility that the other side will be unaware of the unfavorable evidence and fail to request it in discovery.

Overwhelm your opponent

It's easier to overwhelm your opponent if you are a large corporation and defending a class action involving millions of transactions. Simply print the transactions out and deliver the result in a large 18-wheeler. That will keep the plaintiffs busy for months or even years searching through the documents or cost them a great deal of money hiring a specialist firm to scan and index each document into a database.

Unless your client is involved with a business that generates thousands of records, this technique will not be available to you. In addition, discovery rules more and more require that voluminous discovery must be delivered in an organized fashion, and not in a haphazard pile of documents. Today, a judge might even require, *sua sponte*, that the documentation be delivered in optical or magnetic media, especially if the data already exists in that form.

Nevertheless, there may be an opportunity to smother the other side in good faith when the requests actually encompass a large number of documents. For many small businesses, 10 years' worth of financial records may amount to thirty or forty file boxes of paper, the sight of which will strike terror into any paralegal.

Impress your opponent

The best approach to responding to discovery requests is to structure your responses in such a way that your opponent and his attorney will feel that it is in their best interests to settle. The basic philosophy of discovery is that there should be no material evidence known to or in the possession of only one side relevant to the issues raised in the pleadings, so *what* you must disclose to the other side is a matter of law; *how* you present it is up to you.

Yes, your case will have weaknesses, and your opponent may not be aware of all of them. He probably is, however. If he asks for it, he is entitled to unfavorable discovery as well as favorable. If you have thoroughly and diligently investigated your case before you filed the complaint, you have already ascertained (if you are the plaintiff) that your case is winnable and that the facts in your client's favor outweigh the facts in favor of the opposing side. The stronger your case, the less you will need to object, even to requests to disclose privileged material or work product.

Once, defending a criminal case, I informally met with the prosecutor in his office to discuss criminal discovery I had previously requested. When he slid his entire file across his desk and invited me to copy anything I needed, I immediately knew he had an airtight case. A subsequent examination of the prosecutor's file showed that indeed was the case. I advised my client to accept the prosecutor's offer, and he was happy to take the deal.

As much as possible, you should put the strongest facts in your favor first. That means when you are responding to a request for documents, put the documents most damning to the defendant on top, so that the defending lawyer or paralegal will see them first. If it's highly damaging to the other side—something, for instance, that would almost certainly inflame a jury—it might be sufficient by itself to provoke an offer of settlement, but probably not, since most defense attorneys are paid by the hour. In any case, opposing counsel or her paralegal will read the remainder of your discovery responses in the light of what they have already seen. Often their review of subsequent material will be focussed on finding facts that will reduce the settlement amount, rather than defeat your cause of action.

If you are representing the defendant, you may be inclined to wait until you receive the plaintiff's responses to your discovery before you investigate the case and form an opinion on your client's position. Unless this is a routine case, such as insurance defense, you would be better advised to independently verify your client's version of the case, to respond to discovery without later having to wipe egg off your face, or worse.

As a defendant, once you ascertain that the plaintiff has proven all the elements of his cause of action and that you have no defenses that could defeat him, your discovery strategy—by the process of elimination—will focus on mitigation of damages. The "merits" of your side will thus be facts that tend to show that the plaintiff's damages resulting from the actions of the defendant are minimal, as is the culpability of your client, so that he should not be required to fully reimburse the plaintiff for his losses. To the extent you can arrange your responses to emphasize these factors, the lower the plaintiff and his attorney will likely set their settlement target. As a practical matter, a jury, even if instructed otherwise by the judge, will not make a plaintiff whole if it believes that he is mainly responsible for his own injuries or losses.

The format of discovery responses

Most jurisdictions require you to serve upon opposing counsel a written response to requests for production and interrogatories, setting out each request or question and your response below it.

In the case of a request for production, your response will ordinarily be "The plaintiff/defendant will produce the requested document(s)." Other responses include "The plaintiff/defendant is unable to produce the requested document or thing because it is not in his possession or control," or, in the case of a request for privileged material "The plaintiff/defendant objects to the above request because it requests material that is privileged under [cite the rule]."

Scan the discovery requests served upon you and run them through an optical character recognition (OCR) program. That way you or your secretary won't have to retype them. I have been using a Fujitsu ScanSnap scanner for several years, which has proved to be an invaluable time saver. It comes packaged with powerful OCR software adequate for most purposes.

Many of your opponent's requests will turn out to be useful to serve back upon your opponent. If your opponent is an experienced lawyer or happens to work for a law firm with a large library of discovery forms, you may receive some high-quality requests and interrogatories that have been refined by countless lawyers for many years. They cannot prevent you from sending some of their own words back to them. Doing so will give you a deep sense of satisfaction and provide a useful example to draw from in future cases.

Serve supplementary responses

Under FRCP 26(e) and almost all state rules, you are to supplement any discovery response in a timely manner if you learn "that in some material respect the disclosure or response is incomplete or incorrect, and if the additional or corrective information has not otherwise been made known to the other parties during the discovery process or in writing."

Failing to timely supplement will result in the same consequences as failure to timely respond at the beginning.

Chapter Seven

Organizing Discovery Materials

As you begin to accumulate discovery responses and depositions, they tend to pile up in storerooms and filing cabinets. If you have an active litigation practice, they tend to become a problem in more ways than one.

For one thing, the sheer volume of paper and electronic data make it more and more difficult to keep track of all the important information contained in them. It is easy to forget what each witness said, and it is easy to forget a crucial email. Moreover, the size and diversity of the materials you have in your possession—paper, electronic documents, video and sound recordings, even physical exhibits—can make it very difficult to see new ways to connect the dots.

There is often gold to be mined in the wealth of information you have gathered in your course of litigation, if only you can see it from a different perspective.

The traditional method of assimilating all this discovery material is detailed study and note-taking, resulting in exhausted attorneys and three-ring notebooks stuffed with notes and organized as logically as possible. The bigger the case and the more materials, the more numerous the three-ring binders.

One solution to this problem is to create a digest of discovery materials. You can pay someone to compile a digest, but most of the time it is a waste of money. To produce a useful digest the compiler must be familiar enough with the case and your theory of the case, so that she can organize the materials appropriately. This is almost impossible when you hire someone from a temp service or contract with a legal-service bureau.

Most court reporters now deliver their printed depositions along with a computer-generated word index. My experience is that these indices are marginally useful, since they index words, not concepts. The more complex the concept, the greater variety of words and combinations of words that deal with the concept, so a mere list of words and pages is next to worthless.

Database software can aid you in this quest, provided that the probable returns from the case justify the time, money and energy that you must invest in order to get the maximum benefit from the information you put into the system. Given that in order to perform your job as a litigator, you must review virtually all the materials, at least cursorily, the additional task of dictating or typing notes and tags into a computer represents a relatively small addition of time and energy in comparison to what you already must do.

Everything goes in to the digest: depositions, pleadings, exhibits, and anything else that is relevant to the case. Nothing should be left out. It goes without saying that anything going into the digest must be accessible. It does you no good to know that you can prove a fact using an exhibit or a document if you cannot lay hands on the originals or at least copies or photos.

There are many software packages on sale that purport to organize your evidence. They are usually expensive, but if you find one that suits your purpose, it is probably worth the investment.

Once you enter the data into the software, you will normally be able to sort by tag, date, witness, or any other criterion you may think important.

The single most important thing you can do in preparing a digest is to agree upon the keywords or tags that are to be used. Before you begin making entries into a digest program, you and your colleagues (if applicable) should sit down and decide on a list of words to which the contents of all documents should be indexed. One of the problems with using tags in most programs is the lack of consistency. There should be no synonyms among tags or keywords. When you print out a digest, you will want to look in one place for all the documents and exhibits related to a given keyword. You can only do this by determining the keywords in advance and very carefully adding additional keywords when absolutely necessary. Remember that a passage in a deposition may have more than one keyword and if you assign more than one keyword to a passage it will appear in the index with every keyword assigned to it. This is not a defect; it's a feature.

Keywords should be assigned to each significant person, each cause of action, and any other exhibit, object, testimony, or element of a cause of action, as well as any other aspect of the case that you feel is significant. A good digest program will then print out a concordance alphabetically by keyword, with each keyword followed by brief summaries of texts, exhibits or other types of evidence related to that keyword.

If you are handy with a relational database program like

Access, it is easy enough to cobble together a database capable of indexing and printing out a digest by keyword.

Some cases are not worth going to the trouble of preparing a digest, but if you have a complex case involving large sums of money, a digest can not only put you in control of the mountains of paper, but can also suggest new approaches and additional legal theories that could strengthen your claims or defenses.

Chapter Eight

When The Other Side Doesn't Cooperate

There are many different ways in which opposing counsel can be uncooperative. He may simply fail to respond to your requests for discovery. He may produce what are obviously inadequate responses or documents that are not responsive to the requests. He may object to reasonable requests on spurious or invalid grounds. He can make scheduling a deposition difficult.

Sometimes you will encounter an opposing counsel that seems to have been born nasty, whose negotiating technique mainly consists of threats and bullying. He has learned that this technique is particularly effective with insecure attorneys. As a newbie trial attorney not yet familiar with the normal workings of the legal profession or the routines of the discovery process, you will naturally be a little insecure, and thus vulnerable to his threats and bullying. He may—off the cuff—cite a rule that is inapplicable or even non-existent. He may threaten to file a bar complaint or a motion for sanctions for what seems to you an idiotic reason. Because you are not sure of yourself or your legal knowledge or experience, you will probably worry that there exists a possibility that he knows something that you do not.

You will soon realize that the lawyer is blowing smoke, and you need not take his posturing seriously. Be frank. Tell him you are not familiar with the rule, statute, case or legal point, and ask him to put his objection to you in writing.

If he objects in the course of a deposition, make him justify his objection on the record. If his justification seems vague, ambiguous, or evasive, do not hesitate to question him further, then and there, where his objections and arguments will be preserved in a form that a court can later review, if necessary. Bullies are usually reluctant to pull their usual tricks on a video deposition, so you should seriously consider this medicine when you encounter a particularly difficult and obnoxious opposing counsel.

Above all, don't blow your cool. Whoever can make you lose your temper has learned to control you. If you feel your blood pressure rising, call a recess in the deposition and go cool off.

Try to settle your differences

All counsel are required to conduct discovery in good faith. Therefore the rules provide for a gradual escalation in seriousness before the court itself becomes involved.

FRCP 37 and most state rules require the lawyer requesting the discovery to confer or attempt to confer in good faith with the person or party failing to make disclosure or discovery in an attempt to obtain it without court action. Than means that you must contact opposing counsel and inquire as to whether there is some reason for the failure to respond and when you might expect to receive a response. Normally—as a courtesy—you attempt this first with a telephone call. If there is no satisfactory reply or counsel promises to respond and then does not, you should follow up with a "good-faith letter," setting out a brief history of the discovery in the case (by date) and requesting that he respond by a certain deadline.

If opposing counsel responds to your requests with spurious or invalid objections, the proper action is to write her a letter that refutes each objection, citing relevant authorities in support of each point, and renewing your requests for the disputed discovery materials. Never forget that not only must your actions be in good faith and reasonable, but that your good faith and reasonableness should be obvious to any judge or magistrate who may later be deciding discovery disputes that you and opposing counsel cannot resolve between yourselves.

Occasionally, you will encounter an attorney or deponent that is always busy or out of town, no matter what dates you suggest for a deposition. Since most courts limit the time for discovery, usually by specifying a date by which all discovery must be complete, dilatory behavior in scheduling depositions can limit your ability to obtain additional discovery using information you learned in depositions. You can avoid this trap two ways: First, by seeking an agreed order extending the time for discovery, which is the usual method of solving scheduling problems, or second, serving a notice of deposition setting a date. This will flush him out and force him to at least negotiate as to when the deposition will be taken.

File a motion to compel

If opposing counsel does not adequately respond after your good-faith efforts, you may move for an order to compel under FRCP 37(a)(3) or its state equivalent. Incomplete or evasive answers or responses are to be treated as failure to disclose, answer or respond. Filing a motion to compel will please neither opposing counsel nor judge, so it is the nuclear option, to be used only when all else fails.

Chapter Nine

General Office Practices

Although the advice in this section is of a more general character than in the earlier chapters, it covers aspects of your office routines that directly affect how well you handle discovery matters.

Log the flow of documents

Your secretary can begin processing your mail by opening each envelope, putting file numbers on documents when appropriate, and placing the resulting stack in your inbox. She should also put the junk mail in a separate stack, where you can glance at each piece in a hurry. A "Received" stamp containing the date can speed up the process.

Considering the billions of pieces of mail it processes, the USPS does a miraculous job, but it also loses or delays mail on occasion. You do not want to tell a judge that you never received a request for discovery without some solid evidence. "Lost in the mail" is an excuse that judges hear all the time, and they will raise a judicial eyebrow if you use this excuse very often. Proving a negative can be impossible unless you take measures to protect yourself.

The solution: keep separate logs of all incoming and outgoing mail and other documents related to your practice. This logging is best done at the narrow neck of the information funnel (usually the secretary's desk) through which everything passes. You or your secretary can use a computer spreadsheet, note-taking software, or inexpensive spiral notebooks for this purpose. I'm a committed techie, but I used spiral notebooks for years, and they worked fine.

Whoever logs in the mail should record the sender, the date received, the date shown on the envelope that the piece was sent, the name of the case (abbreviated if necessary), your file number (if applicable) and a word or two describing the contents. Note that dates can be altered on a postal meter, so unless there is a date stamped by the Post Office on the face of the envelope, you cannot be absolutely certain of the date it was actually mailed. Similarly, you or your secretary can even log bills and invoices received and payments mailed

Having a reliable contemporaneous record of ingoing and outgoing mail can protect you from sanctions when the Post Office loses an important notice or discovery request. It can bolster your argument for sanctions against the opposite side when you can show that you mailed a notice or request on a certain day. You will be amazed at the usefulness of your logs. My office would typically refer to logs several times a day in the usual course of business.

Log phone messages

Many lawyers use the little pink tear-out phone message slips for telephone messages. Don't. They are easily lost and often accumulate in piles on your desk when you are too busy to answer them right away. In mass, they lack organization and are depressing to look at. As in mail logging, I have used spiral notebooks with entirely satisfactory results.

It is best to avoid taking non-emergency calls from clients; call them back later at a time reserved for that purpose. That will eliminate a source of distractions, which are the enemy of concentration and efficiency. When I call back, I can have the file in front of me and do not waste my time refocusing and getting up to speed. If the secretary can persuade the client to tell her what she is calling about, I can often call the client back with the answer in hand, which saves both of us a great deal of time.

In this scenario, my secretary brings me the call log when I am ready to work through my calls, and as I return calls, I note on the log itself when I responded. Of course, substantive notes about the case itself should be dated and recorded in the case file.

You can, of course, do all this with software, but the most usable software packages for this purpose (like Lotus Notes) are more suitable for large offices and require separate servers. You might try simplenote.com or evernote.com for inexpensive web-based systems, but keep in mind that, while the connections between your computer and the web service might be encrypted, your information on the servers is accessible to the service providers, and thus susceptible to hacking. This also goes for file-sharing services like dropbox.com, as well.

Also, never forget that systems that depend upon the Internet are at the mercy of all those natural disasters and human failings that can throw you offline at the most inconvenient times, so unless there is some substantial benefit of going high-tech over low-tech, the latter is usually safer, more reliable, and less expensive. That is the main reason why there will never exist a completely paperless office, at lease within our lifetimes.

Get your email box to zero by quitting time

The use of the Internet has revolutionized legal communications to the extent that many letters, pleadings and legal documents are transmitted exclusively by email. To stay out of trouble, you must bring your email under control and keep it under control by staying current. A stuffed email box is the equivalent of a cluttered desk, where documents are parked to remind the occupant that something needs to be done about them.

The practice I outline below is only one method of controlling your email. A search on the web will reveal literally thousands of articles on the subject. Ultimately, you must settle upon a method that works for you. Keeping up with email is work, no matter how efficient you are, and it has to be done often, but not so often that it wastes time.

You must also keep in mind that email is inherently insecure. It can be intercepted at many places on the Internet between sender and receiver. For routine messaging, a high level of security is hardly necessary but for sensitive confidential material, there are ethical problems with sending email unencrypted. For extreme protection, you can purchase PGP (Pretty Good Privacy), a commercial program sold by Symantec (http://www.symantec.com), or use for free the GNU Privacy Guard, which is an open-source encryption program using similar algorithms (http://www.gnupg.org). The practical problem with encryption is that both ends of the communication link must use the same encryption software. PGP and GPG are interchangeable, but other encryption systems are mutually exclusive. Once you install these programs and generate keys, the programs are virtually transparent and very easy to use. If you have a particularly important client with particularly sensitive communications, you should consider installing and using high-level encryption software on both your computers that you use to communicate. PGP and GPG are also capable of generating digital signatures that allow a recipient to be certain that the message she received actually came from you, and conversely.

Establish an email address exclusively for practicing law and do not use it for any other purpose. That means that you use it to communicate with courts, other lawyers, clients, and other persons directly involved with your law practice. Do not use it for making purchases, even if they are law-related. Do not use it for anything not related to a specific case. If you give the address to your client, inform him in no uncertain terms that it is for business and not for cute, humorous messages that he received from his buddies. You want to minimize spam, and a lawyer's mailbox is a honey pot for targeted spam.

Maintain a public legal email address that you use for all other purposes. That is the email address that you will give to the bar association, so that the avalanche of advertisements for CLE, books, and other legal services will not distract you when you are doing a sweep of your incoming high-priority mail.

Don't use either of these email addresses for non-legal business.

Depending on your practice, you may find it necessary to check your practice mailbox several times a day. Try to go through your public mailbox no more than once a day.

How to dispose of the actionable or informational legal

emails? Until we arrive at the paperless Valhalla, all legally significant documents and messages should be printed out and filed. Your secretary should log and mark these the same way she logs and marks snailmail. I know many lawyers that leave all their email in their inbox, but they are courting disaster when a hard disk fails or a virus trashes the operating system. Working drafts, on the other hand, can be left on your hard disk and revised on-screen, provided you are comfortable with that procedure. I usually revise and proof short and routine items on the monitor, but print out lengthy pleadings, contracts, briefs and other documents before revising or proofing.

Your goal is to get your inboxes to zero by the end of the day and to process every actionable item into your system so it won't be forgotten or misplaced.

It is a better practice not to delete emails other than spam. Hard disk space is cheap and almost all mail programs allow you to put messages in an archive, so that they are available but don't clutter up your inbox. You can create a mailbox for each case, if you like.

Never forget that notices, messages and orders sometime slip through the cracks; being able to produce a critical message or pleading saved in an archive might be the very thing that rescues your case, or even—under extreme circumstances—your legal career.

Your main hard disk should be backed up daily. You do not want to be finishing up a brief you have worked on for weeks, only to hear the "click...click...click" sound that is the death rattle of a hard disk. Ideally, you will use an online service in the "cloud," as well as media that can be taken off-premises. Incremental backup is fast and reliable and the only practical method of backing up online. Many lawyers use carbonite.com and are very pleased with it.

Concluding Words

I recently mentioned to another attorney that I was writing a book on civil discovery. His response was "Civil litigation *is* discovery; criminal litigation *is* trial."

He was right. Once the parties know all the relevant and material facts, they can usually arrive at a settlement figure that is fair and reasonable. As a result, few civil cases that ask for monetary damages go to trial. Insurance companies, with their verdict-predicting software, usually know what a case is worth long before it is filed.

They will settle, however, only if they believe that you are competent and diligent. If you ever acquire a reputation among members of the defense bar as lazy, sloppy or unethical, you will find that your opponents will prefer to take you to trial, where your weaknesses will manifest themselves in short order. The same goes for civil defense attorneys.

That means that if you elect a civil practice, especially a personal injury practice, you can expect to spend a large percentage of your legal work drafting and serving discovery requests, answering the ones served on you, and attending depositions. It is an honorable and necessary practice that requires diligence, ingenuity, curiosity, and a thorough knowledge of the applicable law. Occasionally, you will have the chance to try a case in court. If you have handled the discovery well, you should be well-prepared to take your case before judge and jury and bring home a just and fair verdict that will please your client, earn you a substantial fee, and establish your reputation in the legal community as a lawyer who must be taken account of.

Appendix A

Instructions To Deponent

(To be given to your client or witness several days in advance of a scheduled deposition)

So you have been advised that your deposition is going to be taken by the opponent. The purpose of these instructions is to inform you what a deposition is, why it is being taken, how it will be taken and pitfalls to be avoided.

1. *What is a deposition?* A deposition is your testimony under oath. You will be asked questions by the opposing attorney and, in some cases, by your attorneys, and the questions and your answers thereto will be recorded by an official court reporter. There will be no judge present, and in all likelihood, the deposition will be taken in the office of one of the attorneys. There is little difference between testimony at a deposition and testimony in the courtroom, except there is no judge presiding and ruling over the matters as they arise. The judge may do so later.

2. *The purpose of a deposition.* The opposing side is taking your deposition for three reasons. The first reason is that they want to find out what facts you have in your actual knowledge

and possession regarding the issues in the lawsuit. In other words, they are interested in knowing now what you know and will testify to at the trial. Secondly, they want to pin your testimony down now, so that your testimony will be the same at the trial, and they will know in advance what your knowledge is. And, thirdly, they hope to catch you in a lie, because if they were to catch you in a lie, they can show at the trial that you are not a truthful person and, therefore, you testimony should not be believed on any of the points, particularly the crucial ones.

These are very legitimate purposes, and the opposing side has every right to take your discovery deposition for these purposes and in this fashion. Correspondingly, you have the same right to take the discovery deposition of the opposing litigant.

3. *Pitfalls to Avoid*

(a) Always remember that either as a litigant or a witness you have no purpose to serve other than to give the facts as you know them. You must give the facts if you have them. You do not, however, have to give opinions, and, therefore, you should not give opinions. Generally speaking, if you are asked a question which calls for an opinion, you attorney will object to the question. However, after his objection, if he advises you to go ahead and answer, and you do have an opinion on the subject, then you may give it.

(b) Never state facts that you don't know. Quite frequently, you will be asked a question by an attorney, and in spite of the fact that you feel that you should know the answer, you do not. Therefore, you will be tempted to guess or estimate what the answer should be. This is a mistake. If you do not know an answer to the question, even though you would appear ignorant or evasive by stating that you don't know, you should nevertheless do so. A guess or an estimate for an answer is almost always the wrong answer and one from which the opponent can show that you either don't know what you are talking about or imply that you are deliberately misstating the truth. Generally speaking, the attorney is in a position to know what the answer should have been. It may very well be that the reason he asked the question was because he knew you wouldn't know the answer but felt that you would be compelled to guess.

(c) Never attempt to explain or justify your answer. You are there to give the facts as you know them. You are not supposed to apologize or attempt to justify those facts. Any attempt as such would make it appear as if you doubt the accuracy or authenticity of your own testimony. Keep your answers short and to the point. Don't volunteer information that is not asked, but fairly answer the specific question you are asked.

(d) You are only to give the information which you readily have at hand. If you do not know certain information, do not give it. Do not turn to your attorney and ask him for the information. Do not turn to another witness, if one should be present, and ask him for the information. Do not promise to get information that you don't readily have at hand unless your attorney advises it. If you know an answer to a question at the time that it is being asked, then you should answer it. Do not agree to look up anything in the future and then supplement the answer you are then giving unless your counsel advises you to.

(e) Do not, without your counsel's request, reach in your pocket for a Social Security card, or other documents. A discovery deposition is to solicit facts which you know and have in your mind and not for the production of documents. If the opposing side is interested in obtaining documents from you, there are other legal procedures with which to obtain them. Do not ask your counsel to produce anything which is in his file at the time, because the same rule applies.

(f) Do not let the opposing attorney get you angry or excited. This destroys the effect of your testimony. You may say things the other side could use to your disadvantage later. It is sometimes the intent of attorneys to get a party excited during his testimony, hoping that he will say things which may be used against him. Under no circumstances should you argue with the opposing attorney. Give him only the information requested and in the same tone of voice and manner that you do in answer to your own attorney's questions. The mere fact that you get emotional about a certain point could be to your opponent's advantage in a lawsuit.

(g) If your attorney begins to speak, stop whatever answer you may be giving and allow him to make his statement. If he is making an objection to the question that is being asked of you, do not answer the question until he, after he has made his objection, advises you to go ahead and complete your answer. If your attorney tells you not to answer a question, then you should refuse to do so.

(h) You may take your time answering a question. Remember, the deposition does not show the length of time you used in considering your answer; it is advisable, however, to answer all questions in a direct and forward manner. The most important thing, if you don't know an answer to a question, is to say so.

(i) Tell the truth. The truth in the deposition or on the witness stand will never really hurt a litigant. A lawyer may explain away the truth, but there is no explaining why a client lied or concealed the truth. The mere fact that you may have sued or been sued by other people at other times on similar claims or even have a criminal record does not destroy the validity of your claim or defense. Deliberately concealing such an action, however, would be devastating to your believability at the trial and would hurt your case immeasurably.

(j) Never joke in a deposition. The humor would not be apparent on the cold, typed record and may make you look crude or cavalier about a serious case.

(k) Be civil, but do not attempt to be helpful to the opposing attorney. Never forget that he is not your friend. Do not volunteer any facts not requested by a question. Such information cannot help your case and may hinder it.

(l) After the deposition is over, do not chat with the opponents or their attorneys. Do not let their friendly manner cause you to drop your guard and become chatty.

(m) Do not try to figure out before you answer whether a truthful answer will help or hinder your case. Answer truthfully. You lawyer can deal with the truth effectively. He is handicapped when you answer any other way.

After you have read all of these suggestions, please write down any questions which you may have and ask them of your attorney prior to the deposition.

Appendix B

Software

PDF Generation

- If you use a Macintosh, you already have a built-in PDF generator. Choose Print from the File menu and the click on the PDF button on the bottom left. You have the option to "Save as PDF."

- If you use a Windows computer, there are several programs that will create PDFs. Both OpenOffice (http://www.openoffice.org) and LibreOffice (http://www.libreoffice.org) can read MS Word files and export them as PDF files. PDFCreator (http://www.pdfforge.org/pdfcreator) can create PDF files from virtually any document.

Encryption

- PGP (Pretty Good Privacy) for Mac and Windows can be purchased from Symantec (http://www.symantec.com) at $175-$323, depending on features.

- GNU Privacy Guard (GPG), which uses the same encryption scheme as PGP can be downloaded free from http://www.gpg4win.org/ (Windows), and http://gpgtools.org/ (Macintosh)

Outlining

There are plenty of outliners available and you should try several in order to find one that suits your mode of organization. Try googling "outliner for Mac" or "outliner for Windows."

- OmniOutliner is probably the premier outliner for the Mac and iPad
  (http://www.omnigroup.com/omnioutliner)
  at $49.99 for the standard version and $74.99 for the pro version. My recommendation is to bite the bullet and buy the pro version.
- Tinderbox
  (http://www.eastgate.com/Tinderbox/)
  ($249.00) is a Swiss Army knife for information, and as such, has an extremely steep learning curve. It is not for the technologically fainthearted, but, once learned, is one of the most useful tools ever invented for the personal computer. Although a Windows version is promised, the release date seems to recede regularly, so for now it is Mac only.
- For Windows, Microsoft One-Note
  (http://office.microsoft.com/en-us/onenote/)
  at $75 for the standalone version is an excellent outliner.
- Microsoft Word has a built-in outliner that integrates nicely with the rest of the word processing.

Backing Up Your Data

- Retrospect for both the Mac and Windows
  (http://www.retrospect.com/)
  is a tried-and-proven backup system in wide use, from

individuals to corporations. Retrospect is not inexpensive, but if you have a lot of data to back up, it will be all you need.

- For backup on my individual Macs, I use Time Machine, which is a part of OS X and comes with no extra charge, and SuperDuper (http://www.shirt-pocket.com/SuperDuper/ superduperdescription.html), which makes a bootable clone of my startup disk which I store offsite. ($27.95)

Made in the USA
San Bernardino, CA
02 January 2016